Istanbul Travel Gu

Istanbul's Kept Secrets Revealed: Your Trusted Guide to an Unparalleled Travel in 2024

By

Cynthia R. Graham

Table of Contents

Chapter 1: Introduction
- *My experience*
- *A Summary of Istanbul in 2024*

Chapter 2: Starting Over
- *Important Travel Information*
- *Transportation Guide*

Chapter 3: Making Travel Plans
- *When is the best time to visit?*
- *Budgeting and Currency Advice*

Chapter 4: Accommodation Guide
- *Top 5 Luxury Hotels with their Prices*
- *Popular Boutique Stays with their Prices*
- *Popular Budget-Friendly Options with their Prices*

Chapter 5: Top Istanbul's Attractions
- *Historic Places Sites*
- *Contemporary Landmarks*
- *Istanbul's Hidden Treasures*

Chapter 6: Highlights of Istanbul's Neighborhood

- *Sultanahmet*
- *Beyoglu*
- *Kadikoy*
- *Besiktas*

Chapter 7: Istanbul's Culinary Delights

- *Traditional Turkish Food*
- *Trendy Restaurants and Cafes*

Chapter 8: Going on a Shopping Spree

- *Traditional Bazaars*
- *Istanbul's Most Popular Modern Shopping Districts*
- *Souvenirs to Look For*

Chapter 9: Experiencing Istanbul's Culture

- *Whirling Dervish Displays*
- *Hamams (Turkish baths)*
- *The Grand Bazaar Experience*
- *Spice Bazaar Expeditions*

Chapter 10: Scenic Landscapes of Istanbul

- *Cruise on the Bosphorus*
- *Retreat on the Prince Islands*
- *Views from Camlica Hill*

Chapter 11: Suggested Itineraries
- *3 Days Itinerary*
- *7 Days Itinerary*
- *2 Weeks Itinerary*
- *Romantic getaways*
- *Istanbul with kids*

Chapter 12: Excursions and Day Trips
- *Islands in the vicinity*
- *Historical Day Trips*
- *Natural Wonders*

Chapters 13: Practical Tips
- *Safety Guidelines*
- *Local Etiquette*

Chapter 14: Istanbul's Popular Events and Festivals
- *Annual Celebrations*
- *Cultural Festivals*

Chapter 15: Quick Reference
- *Emergency Contacts*
- *Useful Phrases*
- *Maps and Navigation Apps*

Hello and welcome to Istanbul

Why settle for a mundane travel when a spectacular one is available? This guide is more than simply a collection of pages; it's a window to the heart of Istanbul, a city that perfectly blends the past and the lively present.

Welcome to Istanbul as you've never seen it before!

Immerse yourself in the enthralling blend of rich history and dynamic modernity that 2024 has in store for you. This expertly designed travel book is your passport to a vibrant city where the echoes of old civilizations blend with the beat of modern culture.

Why should you select this guide?

Because it's more than simply a list of facts; it's a personal voyage through Istanbul, complete with tales, insights, and practical advice to make your visit genuinely unforgettable with:

Exclusive Information: Dive deep into the heart of Istanbul with insider advice and hidden jewels to ensure you have an out-of-the-ordinary experience.

Most recent information: Stay up to date on the newest events, attractions, and trends in the ever-changing Istanbul of 2024.

Unrivaled Exploration: Discover the appeal of renowned landmarks like Hagia Sophia and Blue Mosque, as well as the city's dynamic modern culture at Istanbul Modern and Sapphire Tower.

Culinary Delights: Experience the essence of Istanbul cuisine as we lead you through the scented alleys of the Grand Bazaar and spice-laden lanes of local markets.

Beautiful Landscapes: Let Istanbul's breathtaking splendor captivate your senses as you cruise along the fascinating Bosphorus, escape to the tranquil Prince Islands, and witness panoramic views from Camlica Hill.

Immersion in the Local Environment: Experience Istanbul's spirit through street food safaris, ancient hammam rituals, and Beyoglu's lively nightlife.

This is more than just a guide; it's your ticket to unforgettable memories!

But hold on, there's more! Day visits to historical places like Gallipoli and Troy, practical travel ideas, curated hotel recommendations, and a detailed seasonal events calendar—this guide is your indispensable companion, ensuring that every moment in Istanbul is nothing short of magical.

Don't Pass Up This Opportunity! Now is the time to book your Istanbul adventure!

Join the countless adventurers who have used this book to make their Istanbul fantasies a reality. Every page is a promise—a promise of discovery, delight, and a time-traveling voyage.

Your trip begins with a page turn; allow the enchantment of Istanbul in 2024 to unfold before you. Don't just imagine it; live it with our thorough guide by your side. Istanbul, and your wonderful journey, await you. Get your copy now and make your trip fantasies a reality!

Chapter 1: Introduction

My experience

In the heart of Istanbul's bustling streets, I discovered a world where East and West blended effortlessly, and history murmured tales of long-gone civilizations. It was a journey that went beyond tourism; it was an immersion into the essence of a city that captured me in ways that words can only attempt to describe.

As the first call to prayer sounded through the ancient walls of the Blue Mosque, I was overcome with awe and stood beneath its towering minarets.

Bathed in dawn light, the cerulean tiles created a mosaic of stories spanning millennia. Istanbul engulfed me at that point, a dance of traditions and modernity in every step.

I was captivated by the bright tapestry of colors and the symphony of bartering as I navigated the Grand Bazaar's labyrinthine alleyways. Each stall seemed to contain a piece of Istanbul's history—a mosaic lamp, a handwoven carpet, an elaborate piece of jewelry—all of which told stories of craftsmanship and culture.

On a Bosphorus cruise one evening, the city opened before me like a magic carpet. The cityscape's glittering lights matched the stars above, creating a cosmic dance that left me speechless. The soft lapping of the Bosphorus against the boat's hull revealed the charm of Istanbul, the city of two continents.

The perfume of spices drew me to the Spice Bazaar, where saffron told legends of Silk Road caravans and Turkish delight promised sweet enjoyment. In that bustling market, I not only learned the complexity of Turkish cuisine, but also became acquainted with the heartbeat of daily life in Istanbul.

A day on the Princes' Islands was a peaceful vacation, complete with a boat voyage where seagulls danced in the sea breeze and horse-drawn carriages painted a peaceful scene. Exploring Buyukada, the largest of the islands, was like stepping back in time, a welcome escape from the city.

As I sipped Turkish tea in the courtyard of a medieval mosque, surrounded by the call to prayer, I understood that Istanbul was more than just a destination; it was a tapestry of experiences stitched with threads of history, culture, and genuine friendliness.

Istanbul welcomed me, leaving an unforgettable impression on my soul in every cobbled lane of Sultanahmet, every mouthful of a freshly baked simit, and every stare across the Bosphorus. It wasn't just a city I visited; it became a part of my story, one I share with the world in the hopes of instilling the same enthusiasm and belief in others that Istanbul did in me.

A Summary of Istanbul in 2024

Istanbul in 2024 will be a compelling combination of antiquity and modernity, with historical echoes reverberating against a backdrop of contemporary energy. This metropolis emerges as a captivating tale of cultural richness and architectural grandeur, nestled at the crossroads of Europe and Asia.

Modern Wonders: Explore Istanbul's modern marvels, such as the dazzling Sapphire Tower and the futuristic Kucuk Camlica TV Tower. Istanbul Modern, a modern art landmark, exemplifies the city's devotion to cultural innovation.

Timeless Treasures: Visit the magnificent Hagia Sophia, the ornate Topkapi Palace, and the tranquil Blue Mosque to learn about the legacy of civilizations. These ancient sites convey stories of Byzantine and Ottoman splendor, enabling tourists to enter a real museum.

Culinary Odyssey: Delight your taste buds in the bustling alleys of the Grand Bazaar, where the perfume of spices mingles with the sizzle of street cuisine. In 2024, Istanbul's culinary scene will be a colorful tapestry of tastes, fusing traditional Turkish delicacies with a modern gastronomic flair.

Scenic splendor: Istanbul's surroundings are a visual feast that captivates at every turn, from the fascinating Bosphorus Cruise affording panoramic views of the city's skyline to the calm of the Prince Islands and the spectacular vistas from Camlica Hill.

Local Essence: Immerse yourself in local culture by participating in time-honored traditions such as the Turkish bath (hamam) experience and the vibrant nightlife of Beyoglu. In 2024, Istanbul invites visitors not simply to visit, but to become a part of its unique fabric.

This brief summary only scratches the surface of Istanbul's allure in 2024—a city where the ancient and modern collide, producing a time-traveling experience. Welcome to a year of exploration, where Istanbul welcomes you with open arms to reveal its secrets.

Chapter 2: Starting Over

Important Travel Information

Visa Requirements: Before traveling, make sure to check the visa requirements for your nationality. Many tourists can get an e-Visa online, making the process quick and easy.

Currency and Banking: The Turkish Lira (TRY) is the native currency. Although ATMs are commonly available, it is best to notify your bank of your travel dates to avoid any problems with card transactions.

Language: The official language is Turkish. While English is widely spoken in tourist locations, learning a few basic Turkish words might help you have a better experience and interactions.

Transportation: Istanbul has an extensive public transit system that includes buses, trams, and ferries. Consider obtaining an Istanbulkart for easy transportation. Taxis are also easily accessible.

Weather and Clothing: The weather in Istanbul varies. Check the weather prediction for the dates of your trip and pack accordingly. When visiting holy locations, modest clothes are encouraged.

Safety Tips: While Istanbul is typically safe, it is prudent to use caution in congested locations. Be wary of pickpockets, safeguard your valuables, and heed local advice for a worry-free trip.

Precautions for Health: Make sure your routine vaccines are up to date. It is best to drink bottled water, especially in the heat, and to keep any necessary prescriptions on hand. Check with your doctor about necessary vaccines.

Local customs: Respect local norms and traditions, especially when visiting religious places. Modesty is valued, and it is traditional to remove your shoes before entering someone's home.

Electricity: 230V is the standard voltage, and the frequency is 50Hz. Type F electrical outlets are widespread, so carry adapters if necessary.

Emergency Contact: Save vital contacts in your phone, such as the local emergency number (112), your country's embassy or consulate, and the nearest hospital.

Time Zone: Istanbul operates on Turkey Time (TRT), which is equivalent to UTC+3. Adjust your schedule to account for any time discrepancies in your trip arrangements.

Wi-Fi & Connectivity: Take use of the city's abundant Wi-Fi service in hotels, cafes, and public locations to stay connected. Consider purchasing a local SIM card for mobile data usage during your trip.

Armed with this vital information, you're ready to begin on a smooth and delightful ride through Istanbul's intriguing streets.

Transportation Guide

Public Transportation : Metro: Istanbul's metro system is efficient and well-connected. Lines M1, M2, and M3 cover a large portion of the city.

Trams: utilize the vintage tram to explore the historical peninsula, or utilize the modern tram lines for more convenient transit.

Buses: Istanbul has a well-developed bus network. Buy an Istanbulkart to get discounted rates and simple transfers between buses, trams, and metros.

Ferries and Boats: Take a ferry over the Bosphorus for a picturesque experience. Bosphorus cruises are both functional and scenic, connecting the European and Asian sides of the river.

Taxis: Taxis are readily available. Before beginning the journey, make sure the meter is turned on or agree on a fare. Uber is also available in Istanbul.

Dolmus: Dolmus vehicles are shared taxis or mini buses that travel along predetermined itineraries. A unique and cost-effective mode of transportation, especially over shorter distances.

Walking: In the city center, many of Istanbul's attractions are within walking distance. Wander through Sultanahmet and Beyoglu areas to soak up the colorful vibe.

Cycling: With dedicated bike lanes and bike-sharing schemes, Istanbul is becoming more bike-friendly. Consider riding your bike through the city, particularly along the Bosphorus.

Renting a Car: While traffic might be an issue, renting a car for day trips outside of the city is an alternative. Be mindful of parking and traffic regulations.

Airport Transfers: To get to the city center from Istanbul Airport (IST) or Sabiha Gokcen Airport (SAW), take airport shuttles, taxis, or private transfers.

Apps that are useful: Download transportation apps such as Moovit, Trafi, or IstanbulKart for real-time timetables, route planning, and public transportation information.

Navigation Traffic: Traffic in Istanbul may be crowded, especially during rush hours. Plan your travel schedules properly and consider taking public transportation when seeing the city.

Toll payments on the Bosphorus Bridges: When driving across the Bosphorus bridges, be mindful of toll payments. Two important crossings are the Fatih Sultan Mehmet Bridge and the 15 July Martyrs Bridge.

Emergency Numbers: Keep vital contact information on hand, especially the local emergency number (112), in case of an emergency.

Chapter 3: Making Travel Plans

When is the best time to visit?

The best time to visit Istanbul is determined by your personal interests and the type of experience you seek. Here's a list of the seasons:

Spring (April to June):

- **Weather**: Pleasant temps and blooming sceneries.
- **Highlights**: Beautiful weather for touring, outdoor activities, and strolling through the city's parks and gardens.

Summer (July to August):

- **Weather**: Temperatures range from warm to scorching.
- **Highlights**: include the bustling atmosphere, vivid street activity, and long daylight hours. Ideal for enjoying Bosphorus cruises and visiting the city's outdoor attractions.

Autumn (September to November):

- **Weather**: Mild temperatures with a steady drop from September to November.
- **Highlights:** include pleasant weather, less crowds than in the summer, and the opportunity to attend cultural events and festivals in the city.

Winter (December to March):

- **Weather**: Cool to freezing temperatures with periodic rain from December to March.
- **Highlights**: Fewer people, lower accommodation costs, and a pleasant atmosphere are the highlights. Winter is ideal

for visiting museums, historical sites, and taking traditional Turkish baths.

Special Event Consideration:

- Istanbul Tulip Festival (April): See the city decked out in vibrant flowers.
- Istanbul Music Festival (June-July): A musical delight with a variety of events and acts.
- Istanbul Biennial (even years, September-November): A celebration of contemporary art that draws art lovers from all over the world.

Tips:

- Keeping Away from Crowds: Consider going during the shoulder seasons of spring and autumn if you want less crowds.
- Ramadan: Keep in mind that the dates of Ramadan vary from year to year; traveling

during this period provides a unique cultural experience but may also affect restaurant and activity availability.

Visa Guidelines

Visa requirements for Istanbul vary according to nationality and length of stay. Most people from countries other than the European Union, however, will need to obtain a visa before traveling to Turkey.

Turkish Visa Categories

Visas for Istanbul are offered in a variety of forms, including:

- Tourist visa: The most prevalent sort of visa for tourists, this visa is valid for up to 90 days within a 180-day period.
- Business visa: For business travelers, this visa is valid for up to 90 days within a 180-day period.
- Student visa: For students enrolled in a full-time program at a Turkish university, this visa is valid for the duration of your study.

- Work visa: This visa is valid for the term of your employment and is only available to workers who have received a job offer from a Turkish company.

How to Apply for a Turkish Visa

You can apply for a Turkish visa online through the e-Visa system or at a Turkish embassy or consulate.

To apply online:

- Visit the e-Visa website.
- Create an account and log in.
- Select the type of visa you are applying for.
- Complete the application form and upload the required documents.
- Pay the visa fee.
- Print your visa.

To apply at a Turkish embassy or consulate:

- Visit the Turkish embassy or consulate in your country.
- Submit the required documents and passport photos.

- Pay the visa fee.
- Collect your visa when it is ready.

Required Documents

The required documents for a Turkish visa may vary depending on your nationality and the type of visa you are applying for. However, some of the most common required documents include:

- A valid passport
- Two passport-sized photos
- A completed visa application form
- Proof of accommodation in Turkey
- Proof of financial means
- A return ticket or travel itinerary

Time Required for Processing

The length of time it takes to process a Turkish visa depends on your nationality and the type of visa you are seeking for. A visa, on the other hand, normally takes between 5 and 10 business days to process.

Validity

The validity of a Turkish visa is determined by the type of visa you apply for. Most tourist visas, however, are valid for up to 90 days within a 180-day period.

Extension

If you need to stay in Turkey longer, you can ask for a visa extension through the Turkish Directorate General of Migration.

Overstaying Your Visa

Excessive visa overstaying can result in a fine and deportation from Turkey.

Budgeting and Currency Advice

Local Currency: The Turkish Lira (TRY) is the official currency. Make sure you have enough cash on hand for smaller shops and markets.

Currency Exchange: For better rates, exchange currency at official exchange offices (Döviz Bürosu) or banks. Avoid exchanging money at airports or hotels since rates may be lower.

Credit and debit cards: They are usually accepted in major businesses, but carry some cash with you for smaller vendors and rural markets. To avoid card complications, notify your bank of your travel dates.

ATMs: They are widely available throughout Istanbul. For further security, choose reputed bank ATMs. Check with your bank to see if there are any withdrawal or currency conversion costs.

Budget Accommodation: Istanbul has a variety of lodging options. For a comfortable stay at a variety of price points, consider boutique hotels, hostels, or guesthouses.

Dining Suggestions: Turkish street cuisine is not only tasty but also inexpensive. Explore local eateries and markets for an authentic gastronomic experience that won't cost you a fortune.

Bargaining: This is prevalent, especially in markets such as the Grand Bazaar. Negotiating politely can result in better prices on souvenirs, textiles, and other things.

Public Transit: Use Istanbul's excellent public transit system, which includes buses, trams, and the metro. Consider getting an Istanbulkart for reduced public transportation rates.

Free Activities: Take in the splendor of the city without spending any money. For a low-cost experience, walk along the Bosphorus, explore old neighborhoods, and visit parks.

Museum Pass: If you intend to visit numerous museums and sites, consider purchasing the Istanbul Museum Pass to save money and avoid long lines.

Water and Snacks: Keep hydrated by carrying a reusable water bottle. Snacks from local markets or bakeries are an inexpensive and pleasant pleasure.

Seasonal Factors: Prices may fluctuate depending on the season. Traveling during off-season months may provide more cost-effective lodging and activity possibilities.

Tipping customs: Tipping is usual but not required. In restaurants, round up the total or leave a 5-10% tip, especially if service isn't included.

Emergency Fund: Keep a modest emergency reserve in cash for unforeseen situations or places that may not accept credit cards.

You'll make the most of your Istanbul experience while keeping within your budget if you combine these currency and budgeting recommendations.

Chapter 4: Accommodation Guide

Top 5 Luxury Hotels with their Prices

Four Seasons Hotel Istanbul at Sultanahmet: Situated in the heart of the historic Sultanahmet district, this hotel offers stunning views of the Hagia Sophia and the Blue Mosque.

- Average price per night: $950 - $2,500

Çırağan Palace Kempinski Istanbul: This lavish hotel is located on the banks of the Bosphorus River and features a palace-like architecture and luxurious amenities.

- Average price per night: $1,200 - $3,500

The Ritz-Carlton, Istanbul: This elegant hotel is located in the upscale Nişantaşı district and offers a blend of traditional Ottoman and contemporary design.

- Average price per night: $1,100 - $3,200

Mandarin Oriental, Istanbul: This stylish hotel is located in the Beyoğlu district and offers panoramic views of the Bosphorus River and the Golden Horn.

- Average price per night: $1,000 - $3,000

Raffles Istanbul: This historic hotel is located in the Sirkeci district and offers a blend of Ottoman and Art Deco architecture.

- Average price per night: $900 - $2,700

Please note that these prices are subject to change and may vary depending on the season, room type, and availability

---

Popular Boutique Stays with their Prices

The Pera Palace Hotel: Located in the heart of Beyoğlu district, The Pera Palace Hotel is a historic hotel that has been welcoming guests since 1895.

The hotel is known for its opulent décor, its excellent service, and its central location.

- Price: $400 per night

Çukurcuma Hotel: Located in the trendy Çukurcuma neighborhood, Çukurcuma Hotel is a boutique hotel that is known for its stylish décor and its friendly staff. The hotel is also in close walking distance to many of Istanbul's most popular attractions.

- Price: $250 per night

Hotel Nuru Ziya: Located in the Galata district, Hotel Nuru Ziya is a boutique hotel that is known for its contemporary décor and its rooftop terrace with stunning views of the city. The hotel is also within walking distance to the Galata Tower and Istiklal Avenue.

- Price: $300 per night

The Artisan Istanbul: Located in the Sultanahmet district, The Artisan Istanbul is a boutique hotel that is known for its Ottoman-inspired décor and its hammam. The hotel is also within walking distance to the Hagia Sophia, the Blue Mosque, and the Topkapi Palace.

- Price: $200 per night

The House Hotel: Located in the Karaköy district, The House Hotel is a boutique hotel that is known for its minimalist décor and its cozy atmosphere. The hotel is also in close walking distance to the Galata Bridge and the Istanbul Modern art museum.

- Price: $150 per night

These are just a few of the many great boutique hotels in Istanbul. With so many options to choose from, you're sure to find the perfect hotel for your stay in this vibrant city.

Please note that prices are subject to change and may vary depending on the time of year and availability. It is always best to check with the hotel directly for the most up-to-date pricing information.

Popular Budget-Friendly Options with their Prices

Taksim Hostel: This popular hostel is located in the heart of Istanbul's Taksim district and offers a variety of dorm rooms and private rooms. Prices start at around $10 per night for a dorm bed and $40 per night for a private room.

Sultanhan Hotel: This historic hotel is located in the Sultanahmet district, close to the Hagia Sophia and the Blue Mosque. Prices start at around $30 per night for a single room and $60 per night for a double room.

Miss Istanbul Hotel & Spa: This modern hotel is located in the Beyoğlu district, close to the Galata Tower and Istiklal Avenue. Prices start at around $40 per night for a single room and $80 per night for a double room.

Ramada Istanbul Pera - The Peak Hotel: This hotel is located in the Pera district, close to the Taksim Square and the Istanbul Museum of Modern

Art. Prices start at around $50 per night for a single room and $100 per night for a double room.

Wyndham Istanbul Old City - Celal Aga Konagi: This hotel is located in the Sultanahmet district, close to the Topkapi Palace and the Spice Bazaar. Prices start at around $60 per night for a single room and $120 per night for a double room.

Note that these prices are subject to change and may vary depending on the time of year and availability.

Below are some additional tips for finding budget-friendly accommodation in Istanbul:

- Book your accommodation in advance: Istanbul is a popular tourist destination, so it is important to book your accommodation in advance,especially if you are traveling during peak season.
- Consider staying in a hostel:Hostels are a great way to save money on accommodation,especially if you are traveling solo or on a budget.

- Look for accommodation in a less popular district:Accommodation in Istanbul is generally more expensive in the more popular tourist districts,such as Sultanahmet and Taksim. Consider staying in a less popular district, such as Beyoğlu or Karaköy, to save money.
- Take advantage of deals and discounts: Many hotels and hostels in Istanbul offer deals and discounts, especially if you are booking a long stay or if you are traveling during the off-season.

Chapter 5: Top Istanbul's Attractions

Historic Places Sites

Hagia Sophia (Ayasofya): Empire's Legacy: Originally established as a church by the Byzantine Emperor Justinian I in 537 AD, Hagia Sophia was eventually converted into a mosque under Ottoman authority. It now serves as a museum, displaying an enthralling blend of Byzantine and Ottoman architecture.

Topkapi Palace: Sultan's Residence: For centuries, this grand palace served as the residence of Ottoman sultans. Explore sumptuous chambers, the Harem, and the Imperial Treasury, which houses a stunning collection of antiquities.

Sultan Ahmed Mosque (Blue Mosque): Architectural Wonder:

The Blue Mosque, built in the early 17th century by Sultan Ahmed I, is famous for its magnificent blue tiles that cover its interior. The six minarets of the mosque dot Istanbul's skyline.

Subterranean Splendor: Basilica Cistern (Yerebatan Sarnc): Explore beneath the city to find this historic reservoir established during Emperor Justinian's reign. The columns of the cistern, which are encircled by mysterious reflections, create an ethereal environment.

Süleymaniye Mosque: Architectural Magnificence: This mosque, commissioned by Suleiman the Magnificent and created by the renowned architect Mimar Sinan, is a work of Ottoman art. A hospital, a school, and a hospice are all part of the complex.

Byzantine Mosaics: Chora Church (Kariye Museum) The Chora Church, which was originally a church, is famous for its beautiful mosaics and murals representing biblical scenes. It is a work of Byzantine workmanship and storytelling.

Roman Hippodrome: Ancient Arena: Discover the ruins of the Hippodrome, where chariot racing and other events once delighted Byzantine inhabitants. The Serpent Column and the Obelisk of Theodosius are still standing as reminders of its illustrious history.

Galata Tower: Built in the 14th century, the Galata Tower offers panoramic views over Istanbul. Climb to the observation deck for a spectacular view of the city and the Bosphorus.

Theodosian Walls: Early Defenses: The Theodosian Walls, which stretched for 6.5 kilometers, were built to safeguard Constantinople from invasions. Explore the walls to see the brilliance of Byzantine military architecture.

Istanbul Archaeological Museums: Antiquity in a Time Capsule: This complex, which includes the Archaeological Museum, the Museum of the Ancient Orient, and the Museum of Islamic Art, holds a significant collection of antiquities dating back millennia.

Contemporary Landmarks

Istanbul also has modern landmarks that represent its dynamic and ever-changing personality.

Sapphire Tower: The Sapphire Tower, one of Istanbul's highest structures, dominates the

European skyline. This residential skyscraper is known for its unique, futuristic style and provides panoramic views of the city and the Bosphorus. The Skyride observation platform on the upper floors offers amazing views.

Istanbul Sapphire Shopping Mall: This is a luxury shopping, entertainment, and dining destination located within the Sapphire Tower. Because of its modern architecture and numerous goods, the mall is a popular destination for both locals and visitors.

Istanbul Modern: Istanbul Modern is Turkey's first museum dedicated to modern and contemporary art. The museum, which is located along the Bosphorus, houses a large collection of Turkish and international contemporary art and hosts exhibitions, events, and educational activities.

Zorlu Center: This is a mixed-use development that contains a shopping center, housing, a hotel, and a performing arts facility.

The sleek and sophisticated design of the complex has become a symbol of Istanbul's global lifestyle. It is frequently the site of cultural events and performances.

Kucuk Camlica TV Tower: One of Istanbul's highest structures, the Kucuk Camlica TV Tower, adds a modern flavor to the city's skyline. The viewing decks offer breathtaking views of Istanbul from both the Asian and European perspectives.

Varyap Meridian Grand Tower: Located in Atasehir, the Varyap Meridian Grand Tower is a noteworthy high-rise construction with an original design. The structure includes both residential and commercial areas, contributing to the city's modern urban growth.

Borusan Contemporary: Borusan Contemporary is a contemporary art museum located in the center of the Bosphorus.

The museum is set in a refurbished historic structure

and offers a one-of-a-kind blend of modern art against the backdrop of Istanbul's traditional beauty.

Istanbul Cevahir Shopping and Entertainment Center: As one of Europe's largest shopping malls, Istanbul Cevahir is a modern landmark catering to a wide range of tastes. Aside from its substantial retail offers, the mall also has entertainment opportunities, cinemas, and a diverse range of international and local brands.

Istanbul's Hidden Treasures

Beyond its recognized landmarks, Istanbul reveals hidden jewels. These lesser-known jewels guarantee a more personal relationship with the soul of the city. Let's go on a journey to find the hidden jewels that make Istanbul a magnificent gem in and of itself.

Balat: The Vibrant Quarter

Balat, tucked away on the banks of the Golden Horn, is a vibrant neighborhood.

Explore its small cobblestone lanes, which are lined

with colorful residences, street art, and vintage shops. Balat provides an insight into Istanbul's artistic energy and local life away from the crowded tourist regions.

Kuzguncuk: A Relaxing Waterside Retreat

Escape the city hustle and head to Kuzguncuk, a lovely district in Istanbul's Asian side. This tranquil seaside neighborhood is home to picturesque lanes lined with wooden cottages, quiet cafes, and local markets. It's a peaceful haven that offers a glimpse of Istanbul's more relaxed side.

Suleymaniye Library: A Peaceful Haven

The Suleymaniye Library is nestled among the splendor of the Suleymaniye Mosque complex. With its serene setting and magnificent collection of old manuscripts, this hidden gem is a refuge for book enthusiasts. The tranquil courtyard provides amazing views of the city.

Chora Church (Kariye Museum)

The Chora Church, which was once a Byzantine church, is now home to some of Istanbul's most beautiful mosaics and murals.

While it is not as well-known as Hagia Sophia, its

rich artwork and historical significance make it a hidden gem for art and history buffs.

Yildiz Park: Imperial Peace

Yildiz Park is a natural sanctuary in the center of Istanbul. This royal park, which previously belonged to Ottoman sultans, provides a tranquil respite from the city's bustle. Explore the walking routes and historic pavilions, as well as the magnificent views of the Bosphorus.

Ihlamur Pavilion: Ottoman Elegance

The Ihlamur Pavilion, located in the middle of Besiktas, is a beautiful getaway from the modern

metropolis. This Ottoman-era pavilion oozes tranquility, surrounded by gardens and centuries-old trees. A great place to spend a relaxing afternoon away from the bustle.

Istanbul's Cat Cafés: Feline Charm

Discover Istanbul's obsession with cats in its cat cafés. These quaint establishments provide a distinct blend of coffee, conversation, and the lovely company of resident cats. A hidden gem for animal lovers and those looking for a relaxing getaway.

Fener and Fatih: Genuine Communities

For a real Istanbul experience, visit the Fener and Fatih neighborhoods. Discover Greek Orthodox churches, lively markets, and authentic cafes. These districts offer a taste of Istanbul's unique cultural heritage.

Kucuk Ayasofya (Little Hagia Sophia): A UNESCO World Heritage Site

The Little Hagia Sophia is a hidden architectural gem that is sometimes overshadowed by its grander cousin. The modest stature, detailed features, and tranquil ambiance of this lesser-known mosque captivate   tourists.

Rumeli Hisari: Fortress by the Bosphorus

Built by Sultan Mehmed II in 1452, the Rumeli
Hisari fortress is a hidden historical gem.

Perched on a hill along the Bosphorus, it offers stunning views of the strait and provides a fascinating glimpse into Istanbul's military past.

Chapter 6: Highlights of Istanbul's Neighborhood

Sultanahmet

Sultanahmet is a historic district of Istanbul, Turkey, famous for its rich cultural and architectural legacy. Sultanahmet is a treasure trove of historical wonders, home to some of the city's most renowned attractions, including the Hagia Sophia, Blue Mosque, and Topkapi Palace.

Visitors can meander through the evocative streets, immersing themselves in the area's mix of Byzantine and Ottoman influences.

The Sultanahmet Square acts as a major center, surrounded by museums, cafés, and colorful bazaars, making it an enthralling location for visitors looking to learn about Istanbul's past and present.

Beyoglu

Beyoglu is a bustling district in Istanbul that includes well-known areas such as Istiklal Street, Taksim Square, and Galata. Istiklal Street is a busy pedestrian street surrounded with stores, cafes, and ancient   buildings.

Taksim Square acts as a key gathering place for events and gatherings. Galata's medieval tower provides panoramic views of the city. Beyoglu is a modern and traditional melting pot that draws both locals and tourists.

Kadikoy

Kadikoy is located on Istanbul's Asian side. It is known for its rich history and diversified culture, as well as its distinct blend of traditional and modern elements.

The area is filled with vibrant marketplaces, like the Kadikoy Market, where locals and visitors can shop for fresh vegetables, spices, and authentic Turkish items. Kadikoy is a famous destination for foodies, thanks to its various cafes and restaurants and lively ambiance.

The district also contains historical landmarks such as the Haydarpasa train station and provides breathtaking views of the European side of the Bosphorus. Kadikoy has something for everyone, whether you want to stroll along the waterfront, experience the pulsating nightlife, or immerse yourself in the local artists scene.

Besiktas

Besiktas is well-known for its vibrant atmosphere and varied options. It is located on the city's European side and combines modernity with historical charm. Besiktas Square, flanked by cafes, stores, and colorful street vendors, serves as a focal point.

The famed Bosphorus coastline adds to the attractiveness of the area, offering spectacular views and a popular waterfront promenade. Besiktas also has the well-known Vodafone Park, which is home to the city's cherished football team. Besiktas captivates inhabitants and visitors alike with its blend of entertainment, cultural monuments, and a bustling local scene.

Chapter 7: Istanbul's Culinary Delights

Traditional Turkish Food

Traditional Turkish food in Istanbul is a culinary trip that represents the country's gastronomic heritage's rich tapestry. The city has a wealth of authentic restaurants selling traditional meals such as kebabs, mezes, and pastries. Indulge in world-renowned Turkish kebabs such as Adana kebab or doner, which are frequently served with grilled vegetables and lavash bread. Meze platters feature a variety of tasty snacks including hummus, dolma, and cacik.

With dishes like Iskender kebab and Hünkar Beendi, a creamy eggplant puree topped with pork stew, Istanbul's culinary landscape incorporates Ottoman influences as well. Fresh catches from the Bosphorus may be found in meals such as balik ekmek (fish sandwich) and midye dolma (stuffed mussels).

Don't miss the sweet finale with Turkish desserts like baklava, Turkish delight, and künefe. Throughout Istanbul, you'll discover a blend of traditional flavors and contemporary twists, making the city a paradise for food enthusiasts.

Trendy Restaurants and Cafes

Restaurants

- Raki - This restaurant is located in the Beyoglu district and is known for its modern Turkish cuisine. The menu features a wide variety of meze (small plates), as well as main courses such as lamb shanks and grilled octopus. Prices range from \$20 to \$40 per person.

- Develi - This restaurant is located in the Karakoy district and is known for its traditional Turkish cuisine. The menu features a wide variety of kebabs and stews, as well as traditional Turkish desserts such as baklava and künefe. Prices range from \$30 to \$50 per person.
- Nusr-Et Steakhouse - This steakhouse is located in the Etiler district and is known for its high-end steaks. The menu features a variety of cuts of beef, as well as seafood dishes and sushi. Prices range from \$50 to \$100 per person.
- Eleos - This restaurant is located in the Galataport district and is known for its innovative cuisine. The menu features a variety of small plates, as well as main courses such as roasted lamb chops and sea bass. Prices range from \$50 to \$100 per person.
- Çiya - This restaurant is located in the Kadikoy district and is known for its Kurdish cuisine. The menu features a variety of grilled meats and vegetables, as well as

traditional Kurdish desserts such as halva. Prices range from $30 to $50 per person.

Cafes

- Mangerie - This cafe is located in the Bebek district and is known for its relaxed atmosphere and its selection of coffees, teas, and pastries. Prices range from $5 to $10 per person.
- Māja Coffee and Bistro - This cafe is located in the Cihangir district and is known for its healthy food options and its selection of coffees, teas, and smoothies. Prices range from $5 to $10 per person.
- Petra Roasters - This cafe is located in the Karakoy district and is known for its high-quality coffee and its selection of pastries and sandwiches. Prices range from $5 to $10 per person.
- Coffee Department - This cafe is located in the Nişantaşı district and is known for its wide selection of coffees and its chic atmosphere. Prices range from $5 to $10 per person.

- Çiçek Pasaji Karaköy - This cafe is located in the Karakoy district and is known for its historical atmosphere and its selection of traditional Turkish coffee and pastries. Prices range from $5 to $10 per person.

Chapter 8: Going on a Shopping Spree

Traditional Bazaars

Istanbul's medieval bazaars are enthralling hubs of trade and culture, providing tourists with a sensory feast. The Grand Bazaar, one of the world's oldest and largest covered markets, draws visitors with its labyrinthine pathways lined with bright booths offering everything from carpets and pottery to spices and jewelry. Immerse yourself in the chaos, haggling with friendly shopkeepers.

The Spice Bazaar, also known as the Egyptian Bazaar, is a fragrant sanctuary filled with colorful spices, dried fruits, and Turkish pleasure. You'll come across a rich tapestry of Turkish gastronomic delicacies as you walk through its old streets.

These bazaars are more than just markets; they are living museums. The atmosphere is filled with tradition, and each vendor has a story to tell. From the Ottoman architecture of the Grand Bazaar to the exotic scents of the Spice Bazaar, these markets provide an immersive trip into Istanbul's past and present, making them important stops for anybody experiencing the city's cultural tapestry.

Istanbul's Most Popular Modern Shopping Districts

Istanbul is a shoppers' paradise, with a plethora of sophisticated shopping areas catering to every taste and price. The city provides a unique blend of traditional and contemporary shopping experiences, from posh malls to bustling bazaars.

Nisantasi: Nisantasi is Istanbul's premier fashion district, known for its sleek boutiques, luxury brands, and trendy cafes. Stroll along Abdi İpekçi Caddesi, where you'll find flagship stores of international fashion houses like Louis Vuitton, Chanel, and Gucci. For local designers and unique finds, explore the side streets, where hidden gems await.

Taksim: Taksim is the heart of modern Istanbul, a vibrant hub of entertainment, dining, and shopping. İstiklal Caddesi, the main pedestrian boulevard, is lined with a mix of international chains, local brands, and souvenir shops. Don't miss the historic pasajes (arcades), hidden gems tucked away from the main street, offering a treasure trove of vintage clothing, antiques, and handicrafts.

Bağdat Caddesi: Bağdat Caddesi, on the Asian side of Istanbul, stretches along the coast, offering a mix of high-end brands, local boutiques, and trendy cafes. The tree-lined avenue is a popular spot for leisurely strolls and window-shopping.

Zorlu Center: Zorlu Center, in the Levent district, is a sprawling luxury shopping mall, home to international brands, designer stores, and gourmet restaurants. The mall's sleek architecture and upscale ambiance make it a popular destination for both shopping and socializing.

İstanbul Cevahir: İstanbul Cevahir, in the Sisli district, is one of Europe's largest shopping malls, boasting over 300 stores, an amusement park, and a cinema complex. The mall caters to a wide range of tastes and budgets, with international brands, local shops, and dining options.

Kanyon: Kanyon, in the Levent district, is another popular luxury shopping mall, known for its open-air design and upscale ambiance. The mall features a mix of international brands, designer boutiques, and art galleries.

Mall of Istanbul: Mall of Istanbul, on the European side of the city, is a massive shopping and entertainment complex, with over 350 stores, a theme park, and an aquarium. The mall offers a diverse range of shopping options, from budget-friendly brands to luxury stores.

Souvenirs to Look For

When exploring Istanbul, consider bringing home souvenirs that capture the city's rich culture like:

- Turkish Delight (Lokum): A sweet treat in various flavors, beautifully packaged and perfect for gifting.

- Turkish Tea Sets: Elegant glass or ceramic tea sets, complete with traditional glasses and a samovar, offer a taste of Turkish tea culture.
- Carpets and Kilims: Istanbul is renowned for its intricate handwoven carpets and kilims, showcasing traditional patterns and craftsmanship.
- Spices and Turkish Delicacies: Visit the Spice Bazaar for a variety of spices, saffron, and other Turkish culinary delights.
- Ceramic and Tile Art: Hand-painted ceramics, tiles, and pottery adorned with traditional Ottoman motifs make for unique and artistic souvenirs.
- Evil Eye Talismans (Nazar Boncugu): These charms are believed to ward off evil, and you'll find them in various forms, from jewelry to wall hangings.
- Turkish Coffee Set: Bring home an authentic Turkish coffee set, complete with a cezve (coffee pot) and cups for a true coffee aficionado.
- Calligraphy and Miniatures: Artworks featuring Ottoman calligraphy and miniature paintings reflect the city's historical artistic traditions.

- Copperware: Handcrafted copper items like trays, pots, and utensils showcase Istanbul's skilled metalwork.
- Bosphorus-themed Items: Look for souvenirs depicting the iconic Bosphorus Strait, such as paintings, prints, or ornaments.

Chapter 9: Experiencing Istanbul's Culture

Whirling Dervish Displays

Immersing oneself in Istanbul's cultural experiences is a voyage into the city's rich legacy. The Whirling Dervish ceremonial, a spellbinding Sufi dance that depicts spiritual ascension, is one engaging cultural heritage. Attend a Whirling Dervish performance to see the dancers in their characteristic white robes whirl smoothly to create a trance-like condition while accompanied by mystical music.

Istanbul's historic architecture, such as the Hagia Sophia and Blue Mosque, offers a look into the city's religious and imperial past. Discover the splendor of Byzantine and Ottoman influences at these places.

Traditional Turkish music events highlight the country's unique musical legacy, with instruments such as the oud and ney included. Attend a performance to enjoy the sweet melodies that have resonated around Istanbul for generations.

Furthermore, the city's dynamic street life, bustling bazaars, and local festivals provide an opportunity to mingle with the city's friendly and welcoming residents, delivering a real sense of Istanbul's cultural tapestry. Accept the fusion of ancient and modern inspirations for a really enlightening encounter.

Hamams (Turkish baths)

Immersing yourself in Istanbul's cultural experience frequently entails partaking in the time-honored ritual of Turkish baths, known as "hamams." These bathhouses are more than just a place to cleanse; they are a ritual, a communal activity, and a sensory experience.

You'll be engulfed in a tranquil ambiance in a hammam, which is embellished with fine marble, delicate tiles, and a stunning dome. Relaxation in a heated room is usually the first step, followed by a strong scrub and a soothing massage. The cleansing ritual is stimulating and renewing, and it is based on centuries-old techniques.

Aside from the physical benefits, hamams offer an insight into Turkish hospitality and communal life. It's typical for locals and tourists to share this experience, which fosters a sense of community. A hammam visit's etiquette and traditions reflect the reverence for tradition that pervades Istanbul's cultural fabric.

A Turkish bath is more than just a self-care ritual; it is an examination of history, architecture, and the art of relaxation. It provides a fresh look at Istanbul's cultural riches and the persistent traditions that have molded the city for millennia.

The Grand Bazaar Experience

Exploring Istanbul's Grand Bazaar is a cultural experience unlike any other. Entering this maze-like market is a sensory experience where centuries of history and business mix. The bright tapestry of colors, the hum of bartering, and the heady perfume of spices all combine to transport visitors to another era.

The Grand Bazaar is more than simply a shopping experience; it's a voyage through Turkish history. The architecture, with its domed ceilings and elaborate detailing, evokes Ottoman grandeur. Shops, some of which have been passed down through generations, sell everything from handmade rugs and finely designed pottery to sparkling jewelry and fragrant spices.

Having a conversation with a shopkeeper is a cultural experience in and of itself. Bargaining is a dance in which prices are negotiated with cheerful banter. It's an opportunity to meet locals, hear their tales, and learn about the significance of each item.

The cultural experience is enhanced by sampling Turkish delight, enjoying traditional tea, and marveling at the artistry of artisans. The Grand Bazaar is more than just a bazaar; it's a living museum, a microcosm of Istanbul's rich cultural past. You're not just buying as you negotiate its small alleys; you're also taking part in a centuries-old practice that has created the city.

Spice Bazaar Expeditions

A sensory sensation unlike any other awaits visitors to Istanbul's Spice Bazaar when embarking on a cultural experience. This old market, also known as the Egyptian Bazaar, is a swirl of colors and fragrances that provides a tempting look into Turkish culinary traditions.

As you walk through the Spice Bazaar's bustling alleys, you'll come across kiosks brimming with vivid spices, dried fruits, nuts, and an assortment of Turkish treats. Engage with friendly shopkeepers who frequently tell product stories, giving you a better knowledge of the cultural significance of each spice combination or delicacy.

Immerse yourself in a complex tapestry of aromas by sampling unique spices and enjoying traditional Turkish tea from friendly merchants. The air is filled with the perfume of aromatic herbs, transporting you to the heart of Istanbul's culinary tradition.

Aside from spices, the Spice Bazaar is a mecca for one-of-a-kind items, ranging from handmade soaps to delicate ceramics. The entire event is a celebration of Turkish hospitality and the country's historical role as a cultural crossroads.

Each interaction and discovery in the Spice Bazaar is a cultural exploration, making it a must-visit site for visitors seeking a real experience of Istanbul's lively and savory culture.

Chapter 10: Scenic Landscapes of Istanbul

Cruise on the Bosphorus

A Bosphorus tour in Istanbul reveals a captivating tapestry of magnificent views that merge the city's historic history with breathtaking natural beauty. The Bosphorus Strait, which separates Istanbul's European and Asian sides, serves as the aquatic stage for this enthralling adventure.

Panorama views of prominent locations such as the Dolmabahçe Palace, the old Rumeli Fortress, and the elegant Ottoman-era waterfront houses known as yalis will be provided as the boat glides over the lake. Modern Istanbul set against this historical setting offers a visual spectacle that represents the city's continuous history.

The tour also provides views of the lively waterfront bustle, with fishermen casting their lines and cargo ships deftly traversing the channel. The interaction of sunlight on the lake, particularly at sunset, gives a lovely glow over the city, adding to the whole experience.

The Bosphorus boat delivers an enchanting perspective of Istanbul's different landscapes, whether you select a daytime cruise to appreciate architectural intricacies or an evening cruise to witness the city lit. It's an immersive trip that effortlessly blends the city's past and present, making it a must-see for those looking for both natural beauty and cultural enrichment.

Retreat on the Prince Islands

The magnificent environment of Istanbul continues to the quiet Prince Islands, which provide a peaceful respite from the city's frenetic bustle. This lovely archipelago of nine islands in the Sea of Marmara is accessible via ferry.

The trip to the Prince Islands provides breathtaking views of Istanbul's cityscape and the shimmering seas of the Sea of Marmara. A sensation of tranquility envelops you once you arrive on the islands, particularly Büyükada, Heybeliada, and Knalada. The lack of cars contributes to the tranquil ambiance, with horse-drawn carriages and bicycles serving as the principal method of transit.

The largest island, Büyükada, is known for its lovely Victorian-era architecture, pine-covered hills, and inviting beaches. The renowned Büyükada Clock Tower and the medieval Aya Yorgi Church give cultural richness to the island's attractions.

Exploring the Prince Islands allows you to get away from the hustle and bustle of the city, offering a retreat into nature and a glimpse into Istanbul's old summer resorts.

Views from Camlica Hill

Camlica Hill provides a panoramic view of Istanbul's magnificent scenery, making it a must-see for tourists in search of scenic beauty. This prominent vantage point on the Asian side of the city offers a breathtaking view of the famed Bosphorus Strait, which connects Europe and Asia.

The metropolis unfolds under you as you approach Camlica Hill, exposing an intriguing blend of medieval minarets, modern buildings, and the twisting Bosphorus waterways. The juxtaposition of architectural styles, from antique mosques to modern structures, creates a visually appealing tableau.

Camlica Hill changes into a stunning backdrop at sunset, with the sky ablaze in orange and pink hues, giving a warm glow over Istanbul. The dazzling city lights gradually emerge, lending a magical touch to the twilight scene.

Aside from the visual spectacle, Camlica Hill offers a peaceful respite from the city's hustle and bustle. The well-kept park areas provide a calm setting, inviting visitors to relax and take in the beauty of their surroundings.

Chapter 11: Suggested Itineraries

3 Days Itinerary

Day 1: Explore the Historic Peninsula

- Morning:
    - Start your day with a visit to the iconic Hagia Sophia. Explore its rich history and marvel at the impressive architecture.
    - Walk to the nearby Blue Mosque. Admire its stunning blue tiles and peaceful courtyard.
- Afternoon:
    - Head to the Topkapi Palace, home to Ottoman sultans for centuries. Explore its opulent rooms, courtyards, and the Harem.
    - Wander through the vibrant alleys of the Grand Bazaar. Take your time exploring its diverse shops and perhaps pick up some souvenirs.

- Evening:
  - Enjoy a relaxing evening at a traditional Turkish restaurant in the Sultanahmet area. Try local specialties such as kebabs and mezes.

Day 2: Bosphorus and Modern Istanbul

- Morning:
  - Visit the Spice Bazaar in Eminönü. Immerse yourself in the scents and colors of spices, sweets, and local delicacies.
  - Take a Bosphorus cruise. Enjoy the scenic views of Istanbul's skyline, passing under the Bosphorus Bridge.
- Afternoon:
  - Explore the lively neighborhood of Ortaköy. Visit the Ortaköy Mosque and indulge in a snack from one of the charming local cafes.
  - Head to the Dolmabahçe Palace, a stunning example of Ottoman architecture.

- Evening:
    - Stroll along Istiklal Avenue in the Beyoğlu district. Explore shops, galleries, and enjoy the vibrant atmosphere.
    - Have dinner in the trendy district of Karaköy, known for its hip restaurants and cafes.

Day 3: Asian Side and Cultural Gems

- Morning:
    - Take a ferry to the Asian side of Istanbul. Explore the trendy neighborhood of Kadıköy. Visit the local markets and have breakfast at a traditional Turkish cafe.
- Afternoon:
    - Head to Çamlıca Hill for panoramic views of the city. Enjoy a peaceful afternoon in the expansive park.
    - Visit the Istanbul Modern Art Museum to explore contemporary Turkish art.
- Evening:

- Conclude your trip with a relaxing dinner at a seafood restaurant along the Bosphorus on the Asian side.

---

7 Days Itinerary

Day 1: Historical Peninsula Exploration

- Morning: Visit the iconic Hagia Sophia, marvel at its history and architecture.
- Afternoon: Explore the Blue Mosque and its stunning tilework, followed by a stroll in Sultanahmet Square.
- Evening: Delve into the history of the Basilica Cistern, an ancient underground water reservoir.

Day 2: Topkapi Palace and Bosphorus Cruise

- Morning: Discover the treasures of Topkapi Palace, once the residence of Ottoman sultans.
- Afternoon: Take a leisurely Bosphorus cruise to enjoy panoramic views of the city's skyline.
- Evening: Explore the vibrant Ortakoy district, known for its lively atmosphere and waterfront cafes.

Day 3: Grand Bazaar and Spice Bazaar

- Morning: Immerse yourself in the Grand Bazaar, one of the world's oldest and largest covered markets.
- Afternoon: Wander through the Spice Bazaar, indulging in the aromatic delights.
- Evening: Enjoy a traditional Turkish dinner in the lively Eminonu district.

Day 4: Asian Side and Camlica Hill

- Morning: Take a ferry to the Asian side and explore Kadikoy's markets and vibrant street life.
- Afternoon: Visit Uskudar and climb Camlica Hill for panoramic views.
- Evening: Enjoy a relaxing dinner along the Bosphorus on the Asian side.

Day 5: Chora Church and Fener-Balat

- Morning: Admire the stunning mosaics at the Chora Church.
- Afternoon: Explore the charming neighborhoods of Fener and Balat, known for their colorful houses.
- Evening: Sample local cuisine at a traditional meyhane (Turkish tavern).

Day 6: Princes' Islands

- Full Day Trip: Take a ferry to the Princes' Islands, especially Büyükada, for a tranquil escape.

- Enjoy horse-drawn carriage rides, explore the island's historic sites, and savor fresh seafood.

Day 7: Modern Istanbul and Taksim Square

- Morning: Visit Istanbul Modern Art Museum to experience contemporary Turkish art.
- Afternoon: Stroll along Istiklal Avenue, shop in Taksim Square, and explore the vibrant Beyoglu district.
- Evening: Indulge in the lively nightlife around Taksim and enjoy a farewell dinner.

---

2 Weeks Itinerary

Day 1-3: Explore Sultanahmet District

- Visit Hagia Sophia, Blue Mosque, and Topkapi Palace.
- Stroll through the historic Hippodrome.

- Explore the Basilica Cistern and marvel at its underground grandeur.
- Wander through the Grand Bazaar for a taste of Istanbul's vibrant markets.

Day 4: Bosphorus Cruise and Dolmabahce Palace

- Take a scenic Bosphorus cruise to enjoy panoramic views of the city.
- Visit Dolmabahce Palace, an opulent Ottoman residence.

Day 5: Spice Bazaar and Golden Horn

- Explore the aromatic Spice Bazaar.
- Take a stroll along the Golden Horn waterfront.
- Visit the Rustem Pasha Mosque, known for its exquisite Iznik tiles.

Day 6-7: Asian Side and Maiden's Tower

- Cross to the Asian side, explore Kadikoy's vibrant markets and Moda's trendy cafes.

- Take a ferry to Uskudar, visit the Maiden's Tower for sunset views.

Day 8-9: Princes' Islands

- Spend a day on Büyükada, the largest of the Princes' Islands.
- Explore the island by bike or horse-drawn carriage.

Day 10-11: Taksim Square and Istiklal Avenue

- Experience the lively atmosphere of Taksim Square.
- Walk along Istiklal Avenue, shop in boutiques, and visit Galata Tower.
- Explore the trendy Karakoy district.

Day 12-14: Relaxation and Exploration

- Relax at Hamams like the famous Cagaloglu Hamam.
- Explore Chora Church and its stunning mosaics.

- Wander around Balat and Fener neighborhoods for a glimpse of Istanbul's colorful houses.
- Take a day trip to Sile and Agva for a taste of the Black Sea coast.

Romantic getaways

Day 1: Historical Romance

- Morning: Begin your day with a visit to the Hagia Sophia, a stunning architectural marvel that sets the tone for a day filled with history and romance.
- Late Morning: Stroll hand in hand through the Topkapi Palace, exploring its opulent rooms, beautiful gardens, and enjoying panoramic views of the Bosphorus.
- Afternoon: Share a leisurely lunch at a charming café in Sultanahmet, savoring Turkish delicacies.

- Late Afternoon: Take a relaxing Bosphorus cruise, watching the sun set over the city. Choose a boat with an open deck for a more intimate experience.
- Evening: Enjoy a romantic dinner at a waterside restaurant in the lively district of Ortakoy, with the Bosphorus Bridge illuminated in the background.

Day 2: Bosphorus Romance

- Morning: Visit the Dolmabahce Palace, a symbol of Ottoman grandeur. Explore its exquisite rooms and gardens.
- Late Morning: Take a short walk to the nearby Besiktas district and indulge in a delightful brunch at a cozy café.
- Afternoon: Board a private yacht for a more intimate Bosphorus cruise. Revel in the serenity and breathtaking views as you sail along the strait.
- Late Afternoon: Explore the charming neighborhoods of Bebek and Arnavutkoy, known for their picturesque streets and waterfront cafes.

- Evening: Have dinner at a seafood restaurant in Bebek, enjoying a romantic evening by the Bosphorus.

Day 3: Romantic Retreat

- Morning: Escape to the Princes' Islands for a serene day. Explore Buyukada by horse-drawn carriage, visit historical sites, and enjoy the tranquil atmosphere.
- Afternoon: Have a romantic seaside lunch on Buyukada, savoring fresh seafood.
- Late Afternoon: Take a leisurely bike ride or a romantic walk along the island's shores.
- Evening: Enjoy a candlelit dinner at a cozy restaurant on Buyukada, soaking in the peaceful ambiance.

Istanbul with kids

Day 1: Exploring Old Istanbul

- Morning: Start at the iconic Hagia Sophia, a marvel of architecture and history. Explore its vast interior and marvel at the grand dome.
- Late Morning: Visit the nearby Blue Mosque. Admire its stunning blue tiles and take a leisurely walk around the courtyard.
- Lunch: Enjoy a family lunch at a local restaurant in the Sultanahmet area.
- Afternoon: Head to Topkapi Palace, where kids can be fascinated by the imperial collections, including jewels and historical artifacts.
- Evening: Stroll through the historic Hippodrome area, and if time permits, enjoy a traditional Turkish dinner.

Day 2: Bosphorus Adventure

- Morning: Take a Bosphorus cruise. Kids will love the boat ride, and you'll get to enjoy scenic views of Istanbul's skyline.
- Late Morning: Disembark in Eminönü and explore the lively Spice Bazaar. Let the kids sample Turkish delights and enjoy the vibrant atmosphere.
- Lunch: Try a fish sandwich at the Eminönü waterfront, a local favorite.
- Afternoon: Visit the Rahmi M. Koç Museum, an interactive museum showcasing transportation and technology. Kids can explore exhibits on trains, planes, and maritime history.
- Evening: Head to Ortaköy, a charming district by the Bosphorus. Enjoy a leisurely evening, and let the kids try a "kumpir" (loaded baked potato) from the street vendors.

Day 3: Green Oasis and Playtime

- Morning: Visit the Istanbul Modern Art Museum in Karaköy. The modern art installations may capture the kids' interest.
- Late Morning: Take a taxi or public transport to Miniaturk, a park featuring miniature models of famous landmarks from Turkey and beyond.
- Lunch: Pack a picnic or grab a bite at Miniaturk's cafe.
- Afternoon: Explore Gülhane Park, a green oasis near Topkapi Palace. Let the kids play, and consider a visit to the playground.
- Evening: Visit Istanbul Toy Museum in Göztepe, featuring a vast collection of toys from different eras.

Day 4: Asian Side Adventure

- Morning: Take a ferry to Kadiköy on the Asian side. Enjoy the ferry ride, and explore Kadiköy's vibrant streets.

- Late Morning: Visit Moda Park, a lovely seaside park with playgrounds and green spaces.
- Lunch: Choose a local restaurant in Kadiköy for a taste of Asian side cuisine.
- Afternoon: Explore Bağdat Avenue, known for its shopping and cafes. Visit the KidzMondo Istanbul, an indoor theme park for children where they can role-play various professions.
- Evening: Take the ferry back to the European side, enjoying the city lights.

Chapter 12: Excursions and Day Trips

Islands in the vicinity

Day visits to Istanbul's surrounding islands promise a welcome respite from the city's bustle. The Princes' Islands, which include Büyükada, Heybeliada, and Knalada, provide a peaceful haven just a ferry ride away.

The largest of the islands, Büyükada, enchants visitors with its picturesque horse-drawn carriages, Victorian-era buildings, and tranquil beaches. Stroll through pine-scented lanes, see the landmark Aya Yorgi Church perched on a hill, and dine at waterfront restaurants.

Heybeliada, with its magnificent residences and rich foliage, offers a relaxed atmosphere. Explore the island by bike or on foot, pay a visit to the Naval Cadet School, and relax in one of the island's monasteries.

The smallest of the three, Knalada, is notable for its reddish soil and medicinal springs. Enjoy the island's tranquility, relax in the natural pools, and gaze out over the sea.

These islands provide an insight into Istanbul's past as well as an opportunity to relax in nature. The Princes' Islands beckon with a beautiful blend of history and peacefulness just a short ferry trip from Istanbul's shoreline, whether you're looking for historical landmarks, idyllic scenery, or simply a respite from the city.

Historical Day Trips

Embark on historical day trips from Istanbul to explore the rich tapestry of the region's past. Here are a few notable destinations:

- Ephesus: A visit to this ancient city takes you back in time to the Roman period. Marvel at well-preserved structures like the Library of Celsus and the Grand Theater, providing a glimpse into the splendor of ancient Ephesus.

- Gallipoli Peninsula: Commemorate the historic events of World War I at Gallipoli, where the ANZAC troops landed. Explore poignant memorials and battlefields, reflecting on the sacrifices made during this significant period.
- Troy: Uncover the layers of history at the legendary city of Troy, immortalized in Homer's Iliad. Walk through archaeological ruins, including the famous wooden horse, and absorb the mythical atmosphere.
- Bursa: Known as the first Ottoman capital, Bursa boasts historical sites like the Grand Mosque and the Green Tomb. The city's well-preserved architecture provides a glimpse into the early days of the Ottoman Empire.
- Edirne: Explore the former Ottoman capital, home to architectural gems like the Selimiye Mosque and the Edirne Palace. The city's rich history is evident in its UNESCO-listed structures and vibrant bazaars.

These historical day trips offer a fascinating blend of archaeological wonders, wartime history, and

Ottoman heritage, providing a deeper understanding of Istanbul's broader historical context.

Natural Wonders

While Istanbul is renowned for its rich history and vibrant culture, it also offers enticing day trips and excursions to explore its natural wonders. Consider these escapes:

- Princes' Islands: Take a ferry to the Princes' Islands, a serene archipelago in the Sea of Marmara. No motorized vehicles are allowed, creating a peaceful atmosphere. Enjoy horse-drawn carriage rides and explore the lush landscapes.
- Belgrade Forest: A short drive from the city, Belgrade Forest provides a refreshing retreat. Its wooded trails and picnic areas offer a peaceful environment for nature walks and relaxation.
- Polonezkoy (Adampol): Known as the "Polish Village," this charming area is

surrounded by lush greenery. Explore the picturesque landscapes, enjoy horseback riding, and savor a quiet day away from the city.

- Rumeli Feneri: Located at the northern end of the Bosphorus, Rumeli Feneri offers a serene escape with its lighthouse and tranquil surroundings. Enjoy a coastal walk and absorb the beauty of the Bosphorus meeting the Black Sea.

- Sile and Agva: These coastal towns along the Black Sea boast sandy beaches and picturesque landscapes. Sile's lighthouse and Agva's river make for a perfect day trip filled with natural beauty.

- Darica Zoo and Nature Park: Ideal for families, this zoo is home to a variety of animals in a spacious, green environment. It's a great place to enjoy nature and wildlife.

- Kilyos Beach: For a seaside escape, head to Kilyos Beach on the Black Sea coast. Relax on the sandy shores, take a dip in the sea, or explore nearby cafes.

Chapters 13: Practical Tips

Safety Guidelines

prioritizing your safety is essential when traveling to any destination. Below are some safety guidelines for your trip to Istanbul:

- Stay Informed: Keep abreast of local news and advisories. Stay informed about any potential safety concerns or travel warnings.
- Secure Your Belongings: Be vigilant with your belongings, especially in crowded areas. Use anti-theft devices for bags, and keep important documents secure.
- Use Reputable Transportation: Choose reliable transportation options. Opt for registered taxis, reputable car services, or public transportation from official stations.
- Be Cautious with Street Food: While street food is a delight, choose vendors with proper hygiene practices. Ensure that the food is cooked thoroughly.

- Respect Local Customs: Familiarize yourself with local customs and traditions. Dress modestly, especially when visiting religious sites.
- Stay Hydrated and Sun-Protected: Istanbul can have warm temperatures. Stay hydrated, use sunscreen, and dress appropriately for the weather.
- Emergency Contacts: Save local emergency numbers and the contact information of your embassy or consulate in case you need assistance.
- Avoid Risky Areas: Be aware of your surroundings and avoid poorly lit or unfamiliar areas, especially at night.
- Use Reputable Accommodations: Choose accommodations with positive reviews and a good safety record. Lock your room when leaving and use hotel safes for valuables.
- Learn Basic Phrases: Familiarize yourself with basic Turkish phrases. This can be helpful in communication and can contribute to a positive experience.
- Medical Precautions: Ensure you have necessary vaccinations and carry a basic

medical kit. Know the location of local hospitals or clinics.

- Trust Your Instincts: If a situation feels uncomfortable, trust your instincts and remove yourself from it. Always prioritize your safety and well-being.

Local Etiquette

Understanding and respecting local etiquette is key to a positive experience in Istanbul. Here are some important points to keep in mind:

- Greetings and Politeness: Turks appreciate polite greetings. Use "Merhaba" (Hello) and "Tesekkür ederim" (Thank you) to show respect. When addressing someone, use titles like "Bey" for Mr. or "Hanım" for Mrs./Ms.
- Respect for Elders: Respect for elders is highly valued. Offer your seat to the elderly on public transportation, and use polite

language when speaking with older individuals.

- Shoes Off Indoors: When entering someone's home, it's customary to remove your shoes. Follow this practice in more traditional or private settings.
- Dress Modestly: While Istanbul is diverse, dressing modestly, especially when visiting religious sites, is a sign of respect. Cover your shoulders and knees.
- Use of Right Hand: In Islamic culture, the left hand is traditionally considered less clean. Therefore, use your right hand for greetings, eating, and exchanging money.
- Hospitality: Turks are known for their hospitality. If invited to someone's home, it's polite to bring a small gift. Always express your gratitude for their hospitality.
- Tea Culture: Tea is an integral part of Turkish culture. Accepting a cup of tea is a gesture of friendliness, and it's polite to reciprocate the offer when invited.
- Public Behavior: Maintain a level of decorum in public spaces. Loud or aggressive behavior may be considered disrespectful.

- Queueing: Be patient when waiting in lines. Cutting in line is generally frowned upon.
- Photography Courtesy: Always ask for permission before taking someone's photo, especially in more private or residential areas.
- Ramadan Etiquette: During the holy month of Ramadan, be mindful of those fasting. Refrain from eating, drinking, or smoking in public during daylight hours.
- Tipping: Tipping is appreciated in restaurants and cafes. A tip of around 10% is customary unless service charge is included.

Chapter 14: Istanbul's Popular Events and Festivals

Annual Celebrations

Istanbul is a city that loves to celebrate, and its annual festivities reflect the rich cultural tapestry of the city. Here are some notable celebrations:

- Republic Day (October 29): Celebrating the establishment of the Turkish Republic in 1923, Republic Day is marked by parades, concerts, and events throughout Istanbul. The main ceremony takes place at the Atatürk Mausoleum in Ankara, but Istanbul also joins the nationwide festivities.
- Istanbul Film Festival (March/April): Film enthusiasts gather for this prestigious event, showcasing a diverse range of international and Turkish films. Screenings, workshops, and discussions take place at various venues across the city.

- Istanbul Tulip Festival (April): As spring blooms, millions of tulips adorn parks and public spaces during the Istanbul Tulip Festival. The vibrant colors create a stunning backdrop for the city, and various events celebrate this floral extravaganza.
- Istanbul Music Festival (June/July): Organized by the Istanbul Foundation for Culture and Arts, this festival attracts music lovers with a diverse program featuring classical, jazz, and world music performances at iconic venues like Hagia Eirene.
- Eid al-Fitr: The end of Ramadan is marked by celebrations, family gatherings, and special prayers. Istanbul comes alive with festive lights, traditional sweets, and a joyous atmosphere.
- Istanbul Jazz Festival (July): Jazz enthusiasts flock to various venues across the city to enjoy world-class performances during the Istanbul Jazz Festival. The diverse lineup includes both local and international artists.
- Victory Day (August 30): Commemorating the victory in the Battle of Dumlupınar in 1922, Victory Day features parades, ceremonies, and patriotic events. Turkish

flags adorn the city, and the atmosphere is one of pride and unity.

- New Year's Eve: Istanbul welcomes the new year with lively celebrations, fireworks, and parties. Iconic locations like Taksim Square and the Bosphorus Bridge become focal points for revelers.

Cultural Festivals

Istanbul hosts a vibrant array of cultural festivals that celebrate its rich heritage and diversity throughout the year. Some notable events include:

- Istanbul International Film Festival: Showcasing a diverse range of films, this festival attracts cinephiles worldwide. It provides a platform for both local and international filmmakers to present their work.
- Istanbul Jazz Festival: A musical extravaganza featuring jazz legends and

emerging talents. The festival's diverse program spans various jazz styles, attracting music enthusiasts from around the globe.

- Istanbul Biennial: Held every two years, the Istanbul Biennial is a contemporary art event that transforms the city into a global art hub. It showcases innovative works from international artists, exploring themes relevant to contemporary society.
- Istanbul Music Festival: Celebrating classical music, this festival brings together world-renowned orchestras, conductors, and soloists. The performances often take place in historic venues, adding a cultural dimension to the musical experience.
- International Istanbul Theater Festival: A celebration of performing arts, this festival features a dynamic program of theater productions, dance performances, and experimental works, contributing to the city's thriving theatrical scene.
- Tulip Festival: Annually in April, Istanbul is adorned with vibrant tulip displays in parks and public spaces. The Tulip Festival celebrates the city's historical connection to

tulips and provides a colorful backdrop for springtime.

- International Istanbul Puppet Festival: Focused on puppetry and visual theater, this festival brings together puppeteers from various countries. It offers a unique and imaginative experience for audiences of all ages.
- Istanbul Design Biennial: Exploring the intersection of design, technology, and culture, this biennial showcases innovative design concepts, installations, and discussions. It serves as a platform for dialogue on the role of design in contemporary society.

Chapter 15: Quick Reference

Emergency Contacts

Below are the necessary Emergency Contacts useful for your trip to Istanbul:

Medical

- Emergency services: 112 (ambulance, fire, police)
- Istanbul Metropolitan Municipality Health Services:+90 212 414 44 44
- Istanbul Medical Park: +90 444 66 77
- Acibadem Taksim Hospital: +90 212 257 50 00
- Istanbul Cerrahi Hospital: +90 212 312 10 00

Police

- Emergency services: 112
- Istanbul Police Department:+90 212 529 90 00
- Galata Police Station: +90 212 249 24 10

- Sultanahmet Police Station:+90 212 518 51 00
- Taksim Police Station: +90 212 257 00 00

Other Useful Contacts

- Istanbul Tourist Information:+90 212 263 63 00
- Istanbul Atatürk Airport: +90 212 463 42 42
- İstanbul Sabiha Gökçen Airport: +90 216 585 00 00
- Istanbul Havataş Airport Shuttle: +90 212 198 21 21
- İETT Public Transportation:+90 212 293 00 14

Useful Phrases

Below are some useful phrases you'll need on your trip to Istanbul:

Greetings and Basic Interactions

- Merhaba - Hello
- İyi günler - Good day
- Günaydın - Good morning
- Tünaydın - Good afternoon
- İyi akşamlar - Good evening
- Hoşçakal - Goodbye
- Görüşürüz - See you later
- Lütfen - Please
- Teşekkür ederim - Thank you
- Rica ederim - You're welcome
- Özgür müsünüz? - Are you free?
- İngilizce biliyor musunuz? - Do you speak English?
- Türkçe biliyor musunuz? - Do you speak Turkish?
- Evet - Yes
- Hayır - No
- Tamam - Okay
- Anlamıyorum - I don't understand
- Ne demek istiyorsunuz? - What do you mean?
- Affedersiniz - Excuse me

Asking for Directions

- Nereye gidebilirim? - Where can I go?
- Tuvalet nerede? - Where is the toilet?
- Buraya nasıl gidebilirim? - How can I get here?
- Bu ne kadar? - How much is this?
- Bu restoran nerede? - Where is this restaurant?
- Bu müzeye nasıl gidebilirim? - How can I get to this museum?
- Bu otobüs beni nereye götürür?- Where will this bus take me?
- Sol tarafa dönün - Turn left
- Sağ tarafa dönün - Turn right
- Düz devam edin - Go straight ahead

Transportation

- Bir bilet istiyorum - I want one ticket
- Tek yön bilet istiyorum - I want a one-way ticket
- Gidiş dönüş bilet istiyorum - I want a round-trip ticket
- Öğrenci indirimi var mı? - Is there a student discount?
- Bu trene nasıl binebilirim? - How can I get on this train?

- Bu otobüs hangi durağa gidiyor? - Where does this bus go?
- Taksi - Taxi
- Ücret ne kadar? - How much is the fare?

Shopping

- Bu ne kadar? - How much is this?
- İndirim var mı? - Is there a discount?
- Bu bedenin var mı? - Do you have this size?
- Bu rengi var mı? - Do you have this color?
- Bu ürünü denemek istiyorum - I want to try this product on
- Bu ürünü almak istiyorum - I want to buy this product

Dining

- Menü lütfen - Menu please
- Ne tavsiye edersiniz? - What do you recommend?
- Bu ne kadar? - How much is this?
- Bu yemeğin içinde ne var? - What is in this dish?
- Bu yemeği az pişmiş istiyorum - I want this dish cooked rare

- Bu yemeği orta pişmiş istiyorum - I want this dish cooked medium
- Bu yemeği iyi pişmiş istiyorum - I want this dish cooked well done
- Adınıza hesabı lütfen - The bill,please

Emergency

- Yardım edin! - Help!
- Polis! - Police!
- Ambulans! - Ambulance!
- İtfaiye! - Fire!
- Kayboldum - I'm lost
- Hasta hissediyorum - I feel sick
- Pasaportumu kaybettim - I lost my passport
- Para çaldırdım - I was robbed

Maps and Navigation Apps

Istanbul is a large and bustling city, so having a reliable map and navigation app is essential for getting around. Below are some of the best options:

- Google Maps: Google Maps is a popular choice for travelers worldwide, and it works well in Istanbul. It provides detailed maps, real-time traffic updates, and public transportation directions. You can also use Google Maps to find local businesses and attractions.
- Apple Maps: Apple Maps is a good alternative to Google Maps, especially if you have an iPhone. It offers similar features to Google Maps, including detailed maps, turn-by-turn directions, and public transportation information.
- iIstanbul: iIstanbul is a popular maps and navigation app specifically designed for Istanbul. It provides detailed maps of the city, as well as information about local businesses, attractions, and events. The app also has a unique feature that allows you to see live traffic cameras from around the city.
- CityMaps2Go: CityMaps2Go is a popular offline maps and navigation app. This means that you can download maps of Istanbul before you go, so you can still use the app even if you don't have an internet connection. CityMaps2Go also provides turn-by-turn

directions, public transportation information, and a trip planner.

- Moovit: Moovit is a popular public transportation app that works in cities all over the world, including Istanbul. It provides real-time public transportation information, including arrival times, routes, and fares. You can also use Moovit to plan your trips and save your favorite routes.

Printed in Great Britain
by Amazon

38421120R00069